The 21 Day Ex-Boyfriend Cleanse

THE 21 DAY EX- BOYFRIEND

CLEANSE

...because breaking up is hard to do.

BY ABA ARTHUR

ISBN: 0692430466
ISBN 13: 9780692430460
Library of Congress Control Number: 2015906772
Aba Arthur, Lake Balboa, CA

Dedicated to all the broken hearts...
and those patient enough to help us piece them back together.

The Broken Heart

One billion tiny little pieces...shrapnel which has now been engraved into the sole of his shoe. My heart. My life vessel pumps incessantly. As I lay still, I contemplate its work. Wonder. Its consistency. Its damned power. The pain is never ending radiating from beneath my left breast plate. Make it stop. The same miracle to give me life be the same miracle to make me wish its end. But it keeps pumping, flowing, thriving, giving me seconds, minutes, a lifetime to get over and through this. I will survive. I've lied to myself one billion times in love languages misunderstood by my counterpart. My strength and flaw one in the same. Loyalty. Now, I'm looking at one billion tiny little pieces. Trying to piece back together my life. My future. With each beat of my broken heart, I move on.

Aba

Contents

Introduction

FOR STARTERS, PLEASE LET ME say that neither this Cleanse nor I have the magical powers to mend your broken heart for you. It is designed to give you the tools to avoid wallowing in self-pity for months on end and get back to your life! Time is too precious to waste. I am so sorry you are going through this. It sucks…believe me, I know. That's why I created this process in order to help you to take back control of your heart.

During this Cleanse you need to be prepared to feel. Everything. One of my brilliant sisters once told me that you have to feel your way through the pain to find your peace. Notice it says **through** the pain. Not around it, above it, or attempting to skip it altogether. Meaning if you keep avoiding the pain, bottling it up, drinking it away, or locking it deep down inside, it's going to come bubbling out at some point or another. When it does bubble out, at best you may find yourself snapping at friends and co-workers. At worst, unresolved emotional pain can result in physical illness. We definitely need to be pro-active about that. This process starts when ALL communication with him ends! If you are still playing makeups to break ups, then it will not work. When you *honestly* make the decision that it's time to move on, that's when you should start the process. I would highly encourage that you do not date or entertain any new relationships during this time. Believe it or not, you are vulnerable right now. Even if you ended things and you think you're ok, something about the title and cleansing from your ex got your attention. Listen to that. The last thing we want is for you to hurt someone else's heart, or even worse, have to do this process again with the rebound boo!

With that being said, don't skip any steps. They are all equally as important and must be done in order to have the most effective results. Along with following the process each day, you will find a corresponding blank page for journaling. Use this space to release your thoughts. I suggest reading your exercise for the day in the morning, and journaling your feelings about the day at night. Make sure you stay honest with yourself. Some days there will be a gratitude checklist, in order to remind you of the blessings you have. Though it can be difficult, staying grateful during this time is essential to your healing.

If you are in a situation where communication is necessary (co-worker/co-parent) then you will still follow all the steps. NOTE: In this situation you only speak with him when absolutely necessary. You should not discuss your relationship during the time of Cleanse. Keep the conversation concise, and have others present if possible.

As you'll see throughout this Cleanse, I am speaking to women going through breakups with men. However, I do believe that these steps would benefit anyone grieving a romantic relationship. Everybody hurts right?

If you have a friend you trust enough to hold you accountable during this process then please reach out to them. If not, then honey I'm right here with you!

<u>MY RELATIONSHIP IS OVER...WHAT NOW??</u>

day 1

GRIEVING- Days 1-5:

- Cry, scream, and yell until you're sick of yourself. Get it all out. Call friends if you need to talk about it. DO NOT CALL HIM! Listen to all your sad music on repeat. Drink your favorite wine (if you're of age) and eat all the crap you feel like. Chances are you are in the middle of this stage now. Get it all out because starting in a few days, you will have to put on your big girl undies and be strong.

- In the 5 Stages of Grief*, made famous by Elisabeth Kubler-Ross, we are taught that there is a process to mourning. For each of these 5 days we're going to examine one of the stages. The purpose is to identify what you're feeling and know where you are in your process from now on. Know that you may go back and forth between a few stages, or feel stuck at one point. That is fine. Just make sure that you use this time to FEEL so that you can be present for the rest of the Cleanse.

Day 1:

- **Stage 1- Denial**. Is this you? You're telling yourself that this is temporary. Maybe if you two had a short break, you would both realize the importance of the relationship and figure it out. Maybe he just needs to get advice from someone on what he should fix and then you can work it out. Or my personal favorite…Maybe if he dated someone else briefly, he would see how wonderful you are and come crawling back…because clearly you're the best thing that's ever happened to him right?! This all sounds great for now. I'm so sorry to tell you this, but no. If it is truly over, it's just over ☹ Please note that there is a difference between the denial stage and having makeups to breakups (the process of ending it and making up, then ending it and making up, over and over again.) You have to continue this Cleanse only when you have made up your heart and your mind that you are moving on. Here's your test:

If he calls you right now and says he wants to get back together again, your answer is_____.

If you answered yes, that's ok. If *he* decided to end things, then in order to start this process, you have to get to a place where you realize that your life is better lived loving yourself and being loved by someone who always chooses you. If your answer is yes and *you* decided to end things, then maybe take some time to consider what you truly want from him, the relationship and most importantly yourself. If your answer is no, your Cleanse has officially begun. (*DAY 1 JOURNAL- PG 43*)

day 2

- **Stage 2- Anger**. *Insert numerous expletive filled rants* This is the meat of the hamburger. If the meat (your actions) is not properly cooked (thought through), you are going to eat what you think is a delicious hamburger (act out your thoughts) and you are bound to get sick (saying or doing something you will inevitably regret.) This is the part where you need to practice a bit of self- control. You are angry with him. You are angry with his new woman. You are angry with God. You are angry with a family member or friend. You are angry with yourself. Just angry. You have every right to your feelings. You have every right to be mad because this is not the way it was supposed to turn out. You weren't prepared for this option. I know, believe me. I will just caution you to remember, do not make contact with him. If you have to interact with anyone else that you want to blame, don't discuss this. Now is not the time. You have to be very careful during this stage because your words and actions can have long lasting effects on you and/or the person you're taking it out on. If you find yourself in a fit of anger, please take a moment to step outside of the situation. Take a breath. Make a different choice. Self-control. This is just the beginning of a journey and learning how to control your anger will absolutely make you a stronger, wiser person. I promise we will get to healing and coping methods a little bit later.

For now, recognizing your anger is the first step to moving forward. Please. On to the next... *(DAY 2 JOURNAL- PG 45)*

- **GRIEVING- Days 1-5:** Cry, scream, and yell until you're sick of yourself. Get it all out. Call friends if you need to talk about it. DO NOT CALL HIM! Listen to all your sad music on repeat. Drink your favorite wine (if you're of age) and eat all the crap you feel like. Chances are you are in the middle of this stage now. Get it all out because starting in a few days, you will have to put on your big girl undies and be strong.

day 3

- **Stage 3- Bargaining**. So perhaps if I tell him I threw out those sweatpants he thought were gross, he will find me attractive again. Maybe if I cut off my best friend that he hated, we could give it another shot. If I developed a cancer ending vaccine that would also give us the ability to fly, then maybe he would think I'm smart. We want it so badly to work out that we're willing to make promises which otherwise sound insane. The danger with this stage is that it lies to us. No amount of bargaining will reverse what he said to you. Changing your hairstyle will not magically make you two work. If he comes clean about that one time, it still won't change his character. You can try, but you'll never be able to alter the destined circumstances. We force ourselves to believe that by going to the utmost extreme forms of compromise we can fix the problem. We can't fix it if it's not meant to be. There is light at the end of tunnel.

- It's important to remember that in every relationship there should be a level of compromise. But you need to know the difference between when you have decided to work on an issue together, as opposed to him asking you, or you asking him to change something in the core of who you are. *(Example: He'd love home cooked meals more vs.*

5

you cry too much. OR I would like him to clean up more vs. he doesn't have the level of ambition I need in a mate.)

- Also, some of us have a personality aspect that is not so favorable for us or our loved ones. You will know what this is because you have been told about something you could work on multiple times by multiple people. If this is the case, please take some time to examine it. Find a trusted counselor and take the necessary steps to be your best self. Keep pushing through darling. (*DAY 3 JOURNAL- PG 47*)

- **GRIEVING- Days 1-5:** Cry, scream, and yell until you're sick of yourself. Get it all out. Call friends if you need to talk about it. DO NOT CALL HIM! Listen to all your sad music on repeat. Drink your favorite wine (if you're of age) and eat all the crap you feel like. Chances are you are in the middle of this stage now. Get it all out because starting in a few days, you will have to put on your big girl undies and be strong.

day 4

- **Stage 4- Depression**. Oh the misery. Why??? It hurts. It. Just. Hurts. This stage feels like it will never end. Lack of desire to do anything. Motivation is now a foreign concept. It's like you're sinking in quicksand and you would rather close your eyes and go down than grab the hand of the person standing 2 feet away from you. Because what's the point right? You can't stop crying or you just feel numb. You would rather sleep all day and not answer your phone, or you lie awake at night fighting with the "what if's" and "why's." First, take a deep breath. Let me tell you something: You had a purpose in life before this relationship, and you still have a purpose after. Life does not end when this love does. I know it doesn't seem like it, but this pain will go away. Minute by minute, hour by hour. Keep going through the motions. Keep following the steps we're doing here. Keep waking up. Fake it till you make it. If it gets too hard, call a trusted friend or a counselor. You will make it. (*DAY 4 JOURNAL- PG 49*)

- **GRIEVING- Days 1-5:** Cry, scream, and yell until you're sick of yourself. Get it all out. Call friends if you need to talk about it. DO NOT CALL HIM! Listen to all your sad music on repeat. Drink your favorite wine (if you're of age) and eat all the crap you feel like. Chances are you are in the middle of this stage now. Get it all out because starting in a few days, you will have to put on your big girl undies and be strong.

day 5

- **Stage 5- Acceptance**. Alright, here we are. Your relationship is over… and it sucks. Acceptance doesn't mean that you've learned how not to feel sad, or you're dancing around smiling and handing out lollipops to strangers. Acceptance means that you know your relationship is over…and it sucks. It's like when you watch a great movie in the theatre and at the end, the credits start rolling. You might cry because it was so good but you're not going to yell at the manager and demand that they start it over. At least I hope you don't do that :/ It's because you loved it for what it was and now it's time to move on. You might go see another movie. You might go home and think about the movie you just saw. But you don't sit in the theatre every day for the next 3 months paying to watch that same movie. It's time for us to go home. (*DAY 5 JOURNAL- PG 51*)

ALRIGHT WE GOT THROUGH THE GRIEVING…TOMORROW IT'S TIME TO GET TO WORK ON THE HEALING!

- **GRIEVING- Days 1-5:** Cry, scream, and yell until you're sick of yourself. Get it all out. Call friends if you need to talk about it. DO NOT CALL HIM! Listen to all your sad music on repeat. Drink your favorite wine (if you're of age) and eat all the crap you feel like. Chances are you are in the middle of this stage now. Get it all out because starting in a few days, you will have to put on your big girl undies and be strong.

day 6

REFLECTION- Days 6-10:
- This time is meant for us to reflect on everything our relationship was. It is also meant for us to sit in silence and start taking steps toward the person we want to be. Now that we have defined our grieving stages, make sure that you are able to recognize where you are emotionally. Do this process of recognition daily.

Day 6:
- Make a list of all his CONS. These are all the things you hated about him. The things he did that drove you up the wall. The arguments you had and the things he said to you that were not okay. These are all the moments your inner woman told you "You're better than this!" but you shut her up with 10 million excuses. Write EVERYTHING! Even those things you compromised on. Refer to this list whenever you feel like you want to go back to him, from now until forever...

- *Example*:

I hated this **(small cons)**	**I couldn't live with this forever** **(big cons)**
1. His feet smell	1. He hates my friends
2. The way he chews his food	2. He gets way too drunk
3. He plays too many video games	3. He wants me to try things in bed I'm not comfortable with
4. He would never go to the museum with me	4. The time he said his ex was prettier than me
5. He's not very romantic	5. Sometimes he hits me

WARNING: *One day you may read this list and feel like the things you've written weren't so bad. I beg you to take yourself back to the moment it happened and remember the way it FELT. (DAY 6 JOURNAL- PG 53)*

day 7

- Take 15 minutes at 2 different convenient times of the day. Be quiet and still. Meditate, pray, cry if you need to. This process can continue every day in addition to the other steps as long as you need it to. Focus on what is listed below, and most importantly, believe you already have it! (*Example: Take 15 minutes in the morning, and 15 minutes again at night. Or 15 minutes on your lunch break, and 15 minutes again before bed...etc.*)

- Ask for *SELF- ASSURANCE*: Defined as*...

Confidence
Certainty
Freedom from timidity
Boldness

Example: I ask for self- assurance. I will have full confidence in myself and my decisions. I ask for freedom from self- doubt. I will have certainty. I ask for freedom from timidity. I will have a presumptuous boldness in any and all things that I do. (*DAY 7 JOURNAL- PG 55*)

REFLECTION- Days 6-10:

- This time is meant for us to reflect on everything our relationship was. It is also meant for us to sit in silence and start taking steps toward the person we want to be. Now that we have defined our grieving stages, make sure that you are able to recognize where you are emotionally. Do this process of recognition daily.

day 8

- Take 15 minutes at 2 different convenient times of the day. Be quiet and still. Meditate, pray, cry if you need to. This process can continue every day in addition to the other steps as long as you need it to. Focus on what is listed below, and most importantly, believe you already have it! (*Example: Take 15 minutes in the morning, and 15 minutes again at night. Or 15 minutes on your lunch break, and 15 minutes again before bed…etc.*)

- Ask for *WISDOM:* Defined as*…

  Having the power of discerning and judging properly as to what is true or right; possessing discernment, judgment, or discretion.

- *Example:* I ask for wisdom. That I would find the power to know what is true and right. I ask for discernment. That I will have proper judgment of my actions and the actions of others. (*DAY 8 JOURNAL- PG 57*)

REFLECTION- Days 6-10:

- This time is meant for us to reflect on everything our relationship was. It is also meant for us to sit in silence and start taking steps toward the person we want to be. Now that we have defined our grieving stages, make sure that you are able to recognize where you are emotionally. Do this process of recognition daily.

day 9

- Take 15 minutes at 2 different convenient times of the day. Be quiet and still. Meditate, pray, cry if you need to. This process can continue every day in addition to the other steps as long as you need it to. Focus on what is listed below, and most importantly, believe you already have it! (*Example: Take 15 minutes in the morning, and 15 minutes again at night. Or 15 minutes on your lunch break, and 15 minutes again before bed...etc.*)

- Ask for *HEALING:* Defined as*...

Growing sound
Getting well
Mending
Regaining health
Wholeness
Restoration
Conclusion
Purify
Cure

Example: I ask for healing. That I would be made whole. I will grow emotionally sound and regain health. I envision my restoration. That I will find the conclusion to this pain. I will be pure of heart and walk in my cure. I will be well. (*DAY 9 JOURNAL- PG 59*)

REFLECTION- Days 6-10:

- This time is meant for us to reflect on everything our relationship was. It is also meant for us to sit in silence and start taking steps toward the person we want to be. Now that we have defined our grieving stages, make sure that you are able to recognize where you are emotionally. Do this process of recognition daily.

day 10

- Take 15 minutes at 2 different convenient times of the day. Be quiet and still. Meditate, pray, cry if you need to. This process can continue every day in addition to the other steps as long as you need it to. Focus on what is listed below, and most importantly, believe you already have it! (*Example: Take 15 minutes in the morning, and 15 minutes again at night. Or 15 minutes on your lunch break, and 15 minutes again before bed...etc.*)

- Ask for *PEACE:* Defined as*...

Freedom of the mind from distraction, anxiety, and obsession. Pure tranquility and serenity.

Example: I ask for peace. I will have freedom from this pain. It will no longer distract me from my purpose. I will be free from anxiety and obsession. I ask for tranquility and that I would find serenity. I will find the emotional peace that I deserve. (*DAY 10 JOURNAL- PG 61*)

NOTE: Tomorrow we are moving on, but you can always continue to do this time of reflection along with the other steps if you would like to.

REFLECTION- Days 6-10:

- This time is meant for us to reflect on everything our relationship was. It is also meant for us to sit in silence and start taking steps toward the person we want to be. Now that we have defined our grieving stages, make sure that you are able to recognize where you are emotionally. Do this process of recognition daily.

day 11

DISASSOCIATION- Days 11-14:

*   Time to rid your life of all things him! Hold tight because we're getting to where we need to be ma'am. Note: this step is NOT the same as jumping above or around your pain. This is a conscious decision to reclaim your life and your space both physically and emotionally. You have to remove him from your life so that you can re-learn how to be independent of the relationship.

Day 11:

*   Stop saying his name! Avoid that bubbling urge inside of you to bring him up. Stop telling sad stories to your friends, co- workers and the teller at the bank. If you are asked about him, refer to him as your ex (again...not by his name) Keep the answer brief. Create a standard response to answer why you are not together anymore and stick to it. *(Example: We're not together anymore. I need to do what's best for myself and that means moving on from that relationship. Anyway, how are you doing?)*

*   If you find yourself bursting into tears in a random situation, that is okay. My sister calls these moments "grenades" and we'll get into that a little bit later. If you're in the grocery store and you hear that one song you made out to that one time, allow yourself to feel. Just make

sure you excuse yourself and take a few deep breaths. Remember what you asked for in the time of reflection *(days 7-10: self- assurance, wisdom, healing, peace.)* Resist the urge to come back and discuss it! If you keep giving in, it will never stop. Make this a conscious decision and stick to it...Forever! *(DAY 11 JOURNAL- PG 63)*

day 12

- Start actively avoiding him. If you know he is going to be at a mutual friends' event, skip it. If your brother is still telling you about their phone conversations, ask him to stop. If you desire to have a friendship with him again in the future that is fine, but now is NOT the time. You need to heal separately from him before a healthy friendship can be created. If you don't want anything to do with him ever again, then this is the time for you to kick him out of your mind! You are not giving him control here, you are taking it back. Yes, one day you will attend those events again but please allow this cleansing time of healing before any of that begins. (*DAY 12 JOURNAL- PG 65*)

DISASSOCIATION- Days 11-14:

- Time to rid your life of all things him! Hold tight because we're getting to where we need to be ma'am. Note: this step is NOT the same as jumping above or around your pain. This is a conscious decision to reclaim your life and your space both physically and emotionally. You have to remove him from your life so that you can re-learn how to be independent of the relationship.

day 13

- **"Mind"sweeper** (Clean up day!) - Get rid of all things that remind you of him. Things that will make it difficult to move on. If they are valuable and cannot or should not be removed permanently, then they should be boxed and given to a trusted friend…who will hide them from you. If you lived together, take this time to re arrange furniture and other items in a way that makes you happy. There are two different kinds of women in this world: the kind that needs to throw things away so that she never revisits the memory, and the kind that can box the items up and keep them out of reach from herself. Know which one you are. There is no wrong choice as long as you are being honest with yourself. Remember that no one is watching so do what will bring you healing. Please know that this process may trigger some hard emotions and that is absolutely okay. Just take a minute and *feel* your way through whatever feelings come up, then gather yourself and get back to business ma'am!

- Including but not limited to:

    -Pictures:

- Digital: Put them all into one folder on your computer or device, then erase them. If you need to keep them, transfer the file onto an external drive and give it to a trusted friend…or hide it from yourself.

- Physical photos: It might be therapeutic to cut them up with scissors, box them up and put them away, or just trash them.

-Diary/ Journal talking about him. If it starts to get too difficult, please refer back to the list you made *(day 6)*
-Music
-Jewelry
-Clothing (May include your own panties, bra's, lingerie)
-Sheets
-Any other reasonable things you can get rid of without torching your home!
(DAY 13 JOURNAL- PG 67)

DISASSOCIATION- Days 11-14:

- Time to rid your life of all things him! Hold tight because we're getting to where we need to be ma'am. Note: this step is NOT the same as jumping above or around your pain. This is a conscious decision to reclaim your life and your space both physically and emotionally. You have to remove him from your life so that you can re-learn how to be independent of the relationship.

day 14

- **"Mind"sweeper pt. 2** (Double check your home!) - Do another round of clean up. Make sure you have removed items that still hold memories. Re-visit anything you may have saved from day 13 and really take the time to contemplate whether or not you need to keep it.

- **Grenades:** I won't even lie to you, you're going to be playing "mind"sweeper for a while. Probably the remainder of this Cleanse, and possibly a bit of time afterwards. It extends much further than your home and you need to be prepared for that. You are bound to run into people or places that will remind you of him at times you least expect it. My sister coined the term for these moments "grenades". I've personally experienced grenades during conversations where the subject has nothing to do with him, and then BAM! Something during the convo triggers a memory or a joke he once told me and I'm a sobbing mess. Or you make a wrong turn and drive past that cute little café he took you that one time. Or a guy walks past you on the street and he's wearing the same cologne that your ex used to wear. It's okay, and totally normal. Just excuse yourself...

And breathe.

Recall all the things you asked for during your time of reflection *(days 7-10: self- assurance, wisdom, healing, peace.)* I can honestly tell you that one day it won't even hurt anymore and when grenades pop up, you will smile at the memory and keep it moving. I promise. I just did ☺

(DAY 14 JOURNAL- PG 69)

DISASSOCIATION- Days 11-14:

- Time to rid your life of all things him! Hold tight because we're getting to where we need to be ma'am. Note: this step is NOT the same as jumping above or around your pain. This is a conscious decision to reclaim your life and your space both physically and emotionally. You have to remove him from your life so that you can re-learn how to be independent of the relationship.

day 15

RE-BUILDING- Days 15-20:

- Pick up a new activity. This is something that you did not do with him. If you have a girlfriend that wants to come along then that is great! Otherwise, please feel free to enjoy on your own. You are getting comfortable with yourself so it is fine to go solo. Think about the things that make you feel most alive. What makes you laugh or brings you joy? Try to do something every day until you figure out what you like best and stick with it. Remember that the purpose is not to undo who you were with him, but to rebuild you into a stronger person.

- Ideas for today include: **Body focus**...releasing endorphins and feel good chemicals, yes!

    - Take a bike ride
    - Take a walk while listening to feel good music
    - Yoga
    - Gardening

- The list could go on forever. If you don't like any of the suggestions then look up "fun activities" on the internet. Just force yourself to pick something that fits you and start doing it! (*DAY 15 JOURNAL-PG 71*)

day 16

- Ideas for today's activities include: **Nurture a new skill**...in order to create fresh synapses in the brain. This is about learning new ways to think which don't include your ex.

    - Sign up for a dance class
    - Sign up for a painting class
    - Go to a bookstore and browse or buy a new book
    - Visit a museum
    (DAY 16 JOURNAL- PG 73)

RE-BUILDING- Days 15-20:
- Pick up a new activity. This is something that you did not do with him. If you have a girlfriend that wants to come along then that is great! Otherwise, please feel free to enjoy on your own. You are getting comfortable with yourself so it is fine to go solo. Think about the things that make you feel most alive. What makes you laugh or brings you joy? Try to do something every day until you figure out what you like best and stick with it. Remember that the purpose is not to undo who you were with him, but to rebuild you into a stronger person.

day 17

- Ideas for today's activities include: **Giving back**...step outside yourself and make someone else's needs bigger than your own.

    - Find a church or bible study. Many have Women's groups if you're interested
    - Volunteer (Women's shelter, Homeless shelter)
    - Research and sign up for a program mentoring or tutoring kids
    - Clean out your closet and give away old clothes or shoes (*DAY 17 JOURNAL- PG 75*)

RE-BUILDING- Days 15-20:
- Pick up a new activity. This is something that you did not do with him. If you have a girlfriend that wants to come along then that is great! Otherwise, please feel free to enjoy on your own. You are getting comfortable with yourself so it is fine to go solo. Think about the things that make you feel most alive. What makes you laugh or brings you joy? Try to do something every day until you figure out what you like best and stick with it. Remember that the purpose is not to undo who you were with him, but to rebuild you into a stronger person.

day 18

- Ideas for today's activities include: **Kickin' it in the Kitchen**...food therapy!

  - Find a new or old recipe and try it!
  - Bake a cake/ cupcakes
  - Take a cooking class
  - Make popsicles with your favorite beverage and eat for dessert
    (*DAY 18 JOURNAL- PG 77*)

RE-BUILDING- Days 15-20:
- Pick up a new activity. This is something that you did not do with him. If you have a girlfriend that wants to come along then that is great! Otherwise, please feel free to enjoy on your own. You are getting comfortable with yourself so it is fine to go solo. Think about the things that make you feel most alive. What makes you laugh or brings you joy? Try to do something every day until you figure out what you like best and stick with it. Remember that the purpose is not to undo who you were with him, but to rebuild you into a stronger person.

day 19

- Ideas for today's activities include: **Pamper yourself!**...cause there's nothing better than a little self-love.

    - Treat yourself to a manicure/ pedicure at home or make an appointment at a salon
    - Try a new shade of lipstick. Ask for suggestions at the make-up counter in the mall if you need
    - Go see a movie alone. Yes I know it's intimidating if you haven't done it before but you'll feel great that you tried it by yourself
    - Find a new favorite flower and go buy yourself some. Just because.
    (DAY 19 JOURNAL- PG 79)

RE-BUILDING- Days 15-20:

- Pick up a new activity. This is something that you did not do with him. If you have a girlfriend that wants to come along then that is great! Otherwise, please feel free to enjoy on your own. You are getting comfortable with yourself so it is fine to go solo. Think about the things that make you feel most alive. What makes you laugh or brings you joy? Try to do something every day until you figure out what you like best and stick with it. Remember that the purpose is not to undo who you were with him, but to rebuild you into a stronger person.

day 20

- Ideas for today's activities include: **Reconnecting**...getting back to the core of who you are, with people that you cared about before your relationship.

    - Reach out to those friends you haven't spoken to in a while. Those people who are important to you who may have gotten the back burner while you were in your relationship. Don't feel guilty, we all do it...and don't let anyone make you feel guilty! This is your life and you are starting over. Don't forget your prepared response if you are not yet comfortable going into details about the break up. *(day 11)*

- Please remember that this is about being emotionally healthy and if this person takes you to a place where you are not, then move on. If you would like, invite someone you enjoy to come along on one of your new found activities! Umm, platonic only please. *(DAY 20 JOURNAL- PG 81)*

RE-BUILDING- Days 15-20:
- Pick up a new activity. This is something that you did not do with him. If you have a girlfriend that wants to come along then that is

great! Otherwise, please feel free to enjoy on your own. You are getting comfortable with yourself so it is fine to go solo. Think about the things that make you feel most alive. What makes you laugh or brings you joy? Try to do something every day until you figure out what you like best and stick with it. Remember that the purpose is not to undo who you were with him, but to rebuild you into a stronger person.

day 21

MOVING ON! Last day 21!!!

The thoughts I leave with you...   *Proverbs 4:23*

- You've made it. You are a different person now than you were 21 days ago. You are also going to be a different person from now on than you were when you were in the relationship. Accept the fact that you have a purpose in life past this and push further into it. You are better now for having had this experience. You've learned that love is never easy. That's the truth. Even the good relationships take work. Scratch that. The good relationships take the *most* work. My sweet darling mother once told me "if you didn't have bad days then you wouldn't know how to appreciate the good ones." Stay appreciative in life. It'll bring you long lasting joy.

- Take 10 minutes at the end of this day to have a time of silence and reflection. Make the decision to move on. If from now on you need to take a break from dating, then decide how long that period of time should be and please do so. If tomorrow you feel like going on a date, or a night out with the girls to look for a new boo then be my guest! The point is, today ends an era. Wake up tomorrow morning and program your mind to begin anew!

- If you would like to continue with an activity every day, I suggest continuing your "checklist of gratitude." At the end of each day, write out 5 things that you are grateful for. Try to find the little things in addition to the big ones. Most importantly, I'm proud of you my friend and

I believe you will love again...

"For even as love crowns you so shall he crucify you. Even as he is for your growth so is he for your pruning. Even as he ascends to your height and caresses your tenderest branches that quiver in the sun, so shall he descend to your roots and shake them in their clinging to the earth."

-Kahlil Gibran*

(DAY 21 JOURNAL- PG 83)

day 1
journal

How was today? What feelings came up for you when you took the test? Here it is again…

If he calls you right now and says he wants to get back together again, your answer is_____.

day 2 journal

Did you notice any feelings of anger today? How did you handle it?

day 3
journal

What are some of the bargains you tried to make in your relationship? What are some of the bargains you are trying to make now? In what ways can you be your best self today and/or tomorrow?

day 4
journal

Gratitude Checklist- what are you grateful for?

1. You woke up this morning...which means your purpose has yet to be fulfilled!

2.

3.

4.

5.

day 5
journal

How have your last 5 days been?

day 6
journal

What's your list of his CONS?

day 7
journal

Remember a time *before him* when you felt really confident about something. *Example: A decision you made, or an outfit you wore.* Anything big or small. Write down the story. Live in that moment again...

day 8
journal

Narrow down one time *before him* when you made a really great decision. *Example: A piece of advice you gave a friend, or the way you avoided a chaotic situation.* Anything big or small. Write down the story. Live in that moment again…

day 9
journal

When was one time in your life *before him* that you bounced back from something? *Example: You were disappointed you didn't get what you needed, but you kept going. Someone insulted you and you didn't physically die.* Write down the story. Live in that moment again...

day 10 journal

Think of a time in your life *before him* when you had a peaceful moment. *Example: At the lake by your house, or singing in the shower.* Anything big or small. Where were you? What did it feel like? Write down the story. Live in that moment again...

day 11
journal

How did the day go for you? How many times did you resist the urge to say his name?

day 12
journal

List some places or events that you will need to take a break from...

day 13
journal

Which items were challenging to let go of? Which ones are you still holding on to, and why?

day 14
journal

Gratitude Checklist- what are you grateful for?

1.

2.

3. Your heart is beating. Even though it feels broken, it's still working right this very second.

4.

5.

day 15
journal

What did you decide to do today? Did you enjoy it?

day 16
journal

What are some skills you've always wanted to build?

day 17
journal

What did you do today?

day 18
journal

Did you enjoy today's activity? How was your day otherwise?

day 19
journal

Which activities will you stick with?

day 20
journal

Who did you decide to reconnect with? Were you able to talk about the relationship or did you use a prepared response? How did it go?

day 21
journal

Just write freely. Whatever is in your heart…

REFERENCES

Dictionary.com. *Dictionary.com Unabridged.* 9 February 2015. Website. 9 February 2015. <Dictionary.reference.com/browse>.

Gibran, Kahlil. *The Prophet.* New York: Alfred A. Knopf, 1923. Book.

Ross, Elisabeth Kubler. *On Death and Dying.* New York: Scribner, 1969. Book.

About the Author

*ABA ARTHUR BALWIGAIRE WANTS YOU to know that she is no relationship expert. She has no special training to back up this process she created. However, what she does have is a countless number of break-ups to draw from. Don't worry not just her own...also those from her friends and loved ones who have since crowned her "The Break-up Cleanser." Okay, no she just made that up but it sounds good so she's going to keep it. She created this formula when going through yet another friends' time of heartbreak with her and realized that it worked! She hopes, wishes, and prays that you will have the same success and ultimately find a place where your heart is cherished and happy... ;)

Made in the USA
Middletown, DE
13 October 2015